Taste the Wild Wonder

Taste the Wild Wonder

Poems

John Mark Green

Cover and interior artwork by Beth Little

Taste The Wild Wonder : Poems
1st ed. October 2018
ISBN 978-1725944541

For all who love stars and mysteries.
And for Christy,
who taught my heart to sing again.

Contents

No Other Miracle

Out of the void and vastness
of the cosmos, life emerges;
audacious, improbable.
You and I are here.
No other miracle is needed.

A Brief Awakening

In the vastness of the out-rushing cosmos,
you are but tiny—a warm and pulsing spark.
Against all odds, your birth a brief awakening
from silent eons spent sleeping in the dark.
When you feel your heart swell with wild wonder
at the dazzling diamond chandeliers of night,
know your body was built from ancient stardust
and the universe now sees through your eyes.
So let the breath of sweet gratitude fill you,
as the light of each new day begins.
For this moment itself is a miracle,
and to live it is your privilege my friend.

Witness to the Mystery

You are here
as a witness
to the mystery;
an inhabitant
of the miracle.
When you behold
with startled eyes
and stolen breath,
a curious universe
is admiring itself.
To be bored and jaded
is a crime against nature,
for there's nothing dull
about time's endless parade.
A joyous riot
of shouting color
and dancing sound;
all the myriad ways
life manifests around us.

Go Stand Small Beneath the Stars

Go stand small beneath the stars,
feel the grandeur of your insignificance.
O, grain of sand on a cosmic sea's shore,
savor the foamy waves of glory above.

Drown yourself in the midnight chalice of Erebus,
tasting the terrible beauty of infinite worlds.
Let the night wind whisper sweet nothings,
seducing with its coal-black kisses,
dizzying, and dissolving;
reducing you to raw essence.

Feel in your bones, marrow memories
of the hot blood of the universe,
back when the far-flung was still one.
For a moment, disappear into the tapestry.
Let your cares and concerns fall away.

Go stand small beneath the stars,
learn the humility of your frail existence.

Cocoon

She wears the night
like a mantle of mystery,
its colors stolen from
crow feathers and obsidian.

In sweet solitude of mind,
she listens to wind secrets
and echoes of distant star songs.

Drinking deeply of moonlight magic
and the rich golden hum
from the heart of the universe,
she finds wings and draws strength
in this cocoon of velvet darkness.

Cosmic Dream Girl

I see her in my dreams.
Running through the dark sky,
spilling stars from her pockets.
Long hair blazing behind;
an incandescent comet's trail.
Her footprints—galaxies,
her heart a fiery supernova.
New universes birthed
with each flash of her smile.

Masterpiece

She is a living, breathing work of art.
As audacious as Dali's mustache,
mysterious like a Mona Lisa smile.
As sensual as O'Keeffe's painted petals,
glorious, like a Van Gogh starry night.

Part of the Great Song

There was a silver music to her laughter.
A joyous melody as old as the universe itself.
He recognized the tune, having heard it before—
In stream water slipping over smooth stones,
the delicate shimmer of stars at midnight,
and birdsong symphonies in forest cathedrals.
She was part of the great song of life,
her body an instrument of its expression.

Kiss

Her kiss
dissolves
the universe.

In that moment,
I am unmade
and then reborn.

Permanently Transitory

The cream in my coffee
swirls like a spiral galaxy,
reminding me that the
elements in my body
came from the blazing
hearts of ancient stars,
exploded eons ago.

I look at my hand, holding the mug.
All my skin cells will be replaced
in two or three weeks' time.

Bacteria inhabit my body,
like a high-rise apartment,
outnumbering my own cells
by a factor of ten to one.
Landlord and tenants;
a symbiotic arrangement.

Just who am I, exactly?
The deeper you look,
the blurrier I am
around the edges.
Somewhere within the
patterned dance of molecules,
memories and personality hide.

All of life is hollow.
Such lonely spaces
between the stars,
and vast emptiness
within the atoms
forming me,
and all other things.

Everything appearing solid,
but in truth,
hollow and transitory;
the only constant being change.

And what do we do?
We try to fill the voids
with love, telling ourselves
that it will last forever.

Every five years,
the cells in my body
are completely replaced.
Will those new cells
still love your touch?
Will the echoing atoms
of my heart still be filled
with the same love?
Can my feelings for you
sail safely into the future,
atop such tenuous waves?

Harmony

Our hearts are notes
in Love's great song,
drawn into harmony
by the secret ways
of a playful universe.

Relational Universe

Our reality exists
through relationships.
Space and time,
protons and neutrons.
Nautilus shells,
and spiral galaxies.
Human Chromosome 2,
and William Shakespeare.

Unaware of the deep structure
and persistent patterns surrounding us,
we instinctively replay stories older than time.
Lovers walk the streets of Paris, not knowing
they are fractals of the heart of the universe.

Love's Golden Country

Time has had its rough way
with my flesh and bones.
The swift-passing years
have graven deep their mark.
But you touch something in me
as young as a newborn star,
for in Love's golden country,
we are ageless and immortal.

That Timeless Kiss

Love is a wild thing,
escaping the grasp of time.
Love is governed by its own laws,
reaching into both past and future.
This is a truth that lovers know,
for they have crossed
the threshold of the ordinary,
finding themselves in a place
where time ceases and moments
stretch into eternities.
Have you felt it—
that timeless kiss which love bestows?

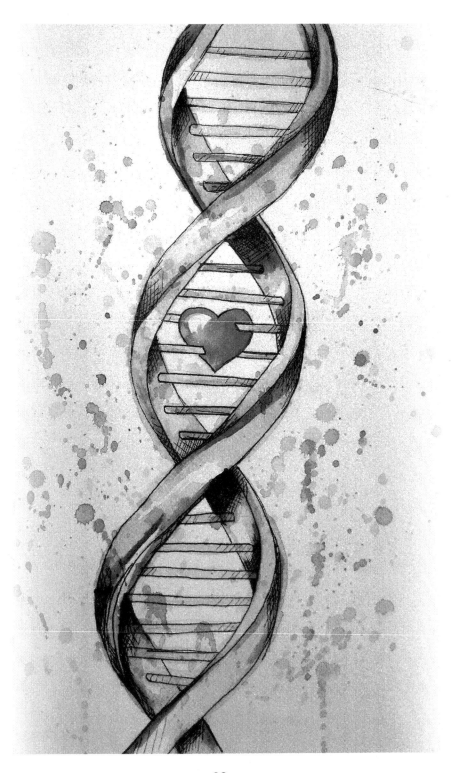

Yūgen

Our breakable hearts,
caught within
a double helix;
forever suspended
between the aching beauty
and inevitable sadness
of this fragile,
wonderful existence.

Such Aching Mystery

You are something beautiful
the universe is expressing.

A colorful thread
in life's tapestry.
A joyous dance of energy.
A small wave, rolling
in the endless ocean.

Such aching mystery hides,
in your stardust-glimmer eyes.

Time is a relentless thief,
but brief moments like these
taste like eternity,
as love makes me one
with you . . . and everything.

Stardust Memories

We are the eyes
by which the universe
beholds its beauty.

Our tiny minds
ponder thoughts
as vast as infinity.

Under ancient light
from distant suns,
our bodies bear
stardust memories.

We are soft machines,
and something more.
Ordered quantum chaos,
fireflies winking in the void.

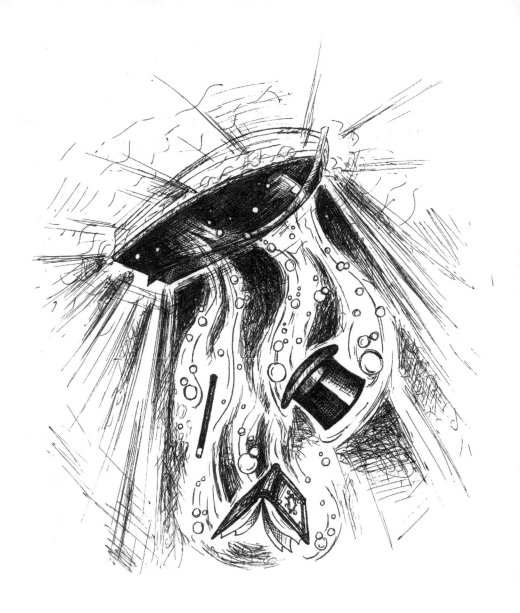

Magic Hats and Leaky Boats

In days of old,
hat makers went mad
from breathing
mercury vapors.

I once had a magic hat
from which I pulled
answers like rabbits.

Learning illusions
from an ancient book,
by skillful sleight of mind
I convinced others and myself.

But when the magic departed,
I was left with only madness.
The hat, I now saw,
was shabby and empty.

Adrift in the universe,
with a sinking heart,
I found my ship of certainty
was infested with termites.
With nothing left to cling to,
I discovered how to float.

Sanity returned,
and my eyes opened
to the magic
all around me.

Reality's rabbit hole
is far stranger
than any fiction
Alice discovered,
and keys shaped
like question marks
will open almost any door.

The End of the Affair

I had a long and complicated
affair with Certainty,
but she had a bad habit
of making things up.
Eventually we parted ways.

Now I'm in a committed relationship
with my new love, Curiosity.
She captivates me
with her beautiful questions,
astonishing me with her honest inquiry.

I've decided I don't need all the answers.
I'll follow wherever Curiosity leads.
Some mysteries will be uncovered along the way,
but it's the thrill of the chase that matters most.

The Endless Thirst

In the quest for understanding,
there is always room for mystery.
More layers of reality to unpeel,
tempting discoveries, just beyond reach.
The endless thirst for knowing
will never be fully satisfied.
Learning how much we don't know.
Seeing the world with adventurous eyes.

Fumbling for Truth

I crave understanding
and hunger for insight.
My ever-longing heart
always reaches for more.

I trace delicate mysteries
with clumsy fingers,
a blind man touching
the beautiful face of forever.

Lady Mystery

Lady Mystery
seductively twirls
her diaphanous skirt.
Through the parted
doors of perception,
a tempting glimpse;
thigh of the unknown,
curves of the unexplained.
Lacey constellation lingerie——
the irresistible allure of the universe.
Galaxy eyes daring me to explore.
Secrets yet to be undressed;
the flesh of truth laid bare.

The Unexpected Beautiful

Fling wide your heart
to the unexpected beautiful.
It hides in plain sight,
amidst everyday things.

So often we're numb
to the wonder around us,
like blinded workhorses
enslaved to routine.

Drink thirstily of the world,
with child-hearted rejoicing.
Be curious and playful;
let your soul's stale lungs
breathe deeply once again.

Inspiratus

Sometimes I can feel it—
that wind beyond the stars.
Silently slipping through this world,
swaying wind chime hearts.

Poet

Perhaps a poet is someone
who attempts to describe
the faint scent of music
carried on an evening breeze.
A painter capturing the sound
of a dream dissolved by waking.
A linguist translating inscriptions
in a lost language found only on
ancient temple walls of the heart.

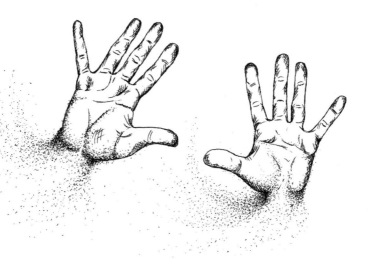

The Burning Man

I am a wick
through which
the oil of words
is drawn from
some other place.

An invisible hand
strikes fire, and I
burn beautifully.

A Trembling Quiet

Have you felt them?
Those rare moments which disrupt
the mindless motions of our lives,
leaving us breathless.

Melting away boundaries
of body and mind,
they dissolve us
into the divine
union of raw experience.

Awestruck
and reverentially silent,
we enter stained-glass awareness.
A sacred encounter
with that mysterious moment
when the universe becomes numinous.

Afterwards, the memory
of something unutterable
lingers within us.
A trembling quiet,
like the resonant moment
after a church bell has rung.

All These Things Shall Be Dissolved

I remember, as a child,
the simple delight
of gazing up at dizzy heights
of a cloud-laden winter sky,
fat flakes lazily falling
like a paratrooper invasion.

I could not look for long.
Falling snow caught in my lashes,
blurring my vision like tears
to be brushed away
with red woolen mittens.

Open-mouthed,
I caught the cold
crystalline perfection
of snow on my extended tongue.
By the warmth of my body,
dissolved and then gone.

We are snowflakes, melting
on the tongue of the universe.

In the Space Between

Exquisite beauty
is often hidden
in life's fragile,
fleeting moments.
The quivering silence
between lightning flash
and thunderclap.
A fiery autumn leaf's
fluttering descent
from branch to cold earth.
Breathless lips
parted,
poised to kiss.
The space between
this heartbeat
and the next.
The evanescent years
between birth and death.

The Secret of Small Things

Each day offers moments of joy,
ripened berries on life's vine.
Invitations awaiting your attention.

Taste them, savoring
bursts of rich sweetness.
Nourish yourself in this way.
Let the slow golden warmth
of happiness fill you.

Learn the secret of small things.

Listen for the Lost Song

In certain moments
of deep stillness,
you may hear it—
a faint melody
of aching beauty,
drifting softly in
through a window
left open
in some back room
of your heart.

The Ruins of Time

Lovers steal fire
amidst the ruins of time.
The gray-bearded nebulae
convene their star chamber.

A small spider works all night,
weaving a web of ancient design,
and I write words which leap
like fish in the moonlight,
silver from the lake of my soul.

Treasures of the Barren Sea

In cars fueled by refined blood
drawn from the hidden veins
of Earth's ancient heart,
we drove across a desert,
which long, long ago, was once a sea.

We searched for shark tooth fossils,
scattered in the shifting sands.
A maze of canyons and formations,
under the sky's vast blue expanse;
graveyard of the Jurassic and Cretaceous.

I'd never yet uncovered
any ancient incisors,
only witnessed them
in the possession of others.
Pointed, smooth, and dark,
shaped like deadly little hearts.

Not even fifteen minutes in,
I heard a friend say
"What do you think this is?"
And of course, it was a shark tooth.
Beginners luck.

Passing it around,
we memorized the shape,
eagerly fanning out
and searching, but in vain.
No one else found any that day.

The desert holds its secrets,
revealing only what it wishes,
when it decides the time is right.

A few years later,
hikers in that same area
would stumble upon
the fossilized skeleton
of a 20-foot-long plesiosaur,
revealed after 93 million years.
But on the day of our search,
all we were given was just one tooth.

Portals

Mysterious doors
standing in fields,
leading to other worlds.

Hand-drawn maps
folded carefully inside
worn leather-bound books.

Antique tincture bottles
with unreadable labels.
Thick, clouded glass.
A pulsing glow within.

Portals to adventure.

Apply Within

Seeking the ideal companion:
must love random adventures,
exploring used bookstores,
philosophical conversations,
long walks in the woods,
and the occasional trip
to alternate universes.

Craigslist 2090

For sale:
Time machine.
Low miles, runs great.
Clean title.
Flux Capacitor recently replaced.
Some cosmetic damage from T-Rex bite marks.
Baby on the way, wife says I have to sell.
Serious inquiries only.

Stones of Remembrance

My grandfather's Kentucky farm—
treasure trove of my childhood.
Hidden in the dirt behind the garage,
thick pieces of oddly colored glass;
fragments of old-fashioned bottles
waiting like priceless buried gems.
Plowed tobacco fields; time excavated.
Indian arrowheads, sharp-edged still;
traces of hunter-warriors long gone.
Over the back fence, up the hill,
broken limestone slabs riddled
with the whiteness of tiny shells,
bones, and sea things unknown.
Scattered gears and springs
from the blind watchmaker's toolbox.
Stone tablets—
not commandments
of some Bronze-Age tribal god,
but memories of the ancient Earth
made manifest in Fulton Shale.
My fingers touched relics
from a misted distant past,
and my sacred imagination soared.

Pop Art

Long before Plato
told his cave story,
anonymous artists
painted Lascaux's
shadowy grotto walls.
They got Andy Warhol's
fifteen minutes of fame,
albeit 17,000 years late.
And although that quote
might not even be Warhol's words,
he's still famous for it anyway.

The Past is Present

Julius Caesar's dying breath stirs
a butterfly's wings two millennia later.

Millions now carry the genetic signature
of Genghis Khan's prolific pen.

The Arctic melts, ancient viruses rising
like silent warriors from icy tombs.

Before the Curtain Call

Dawn's arson sets the sky ablaze,
spreading like a ravenous wildfire.
An invitation to awaken
from the sleep that is not yet final.
Our pale blue dot spins
against a starry backdrop.
And in the invisible hands
of the grand magician Time,
our days burn like flash paper.
Flaring brilliance, then ashes;
marking our brief moment on stage.

Escaping the Asylum

The open highway,
a thread unravelling
the straight jacket confinement
of concrete canyons and rush hour insanity.
I feel my heart open like a lover's smile,
in harmony with the widening horizon.

Sedona Moment

Red rock cathedrals rise.
Majestic sentinels standing
against an infinite cobalt sky.

An unseen river wraps itself
with a lushly verdant mantle.
Treetops swaying,
moved by windsong.
A graceful dance
between shadow and light.

Hidden roots
drink deeply of snowmelt,
tasting distant mountaintops.

My love and I, side by side.
Writing poetry
to the sound of icy waters
tumbling over time-worn stones.

A curious dragonfly
boldly alights on my knee
while I try to find a way
to make this moment last forever.

A Day in Poetry

Sunrise,
the sky opens.
An iridescent oyster shell
revealing its blazing pearl.

Red rock cathedrals,
evoking awe,
Notre-Dame pales.

In the blue sky vault,
tiny black dots fly;
winged thieves
stealing their freedom.

Dewy meadow at dusk.
Lonely fireflies
winking their pickup lines.

Violinist crickets scraping
rusty music from their wings,
somewhere out in the darkness.

Bottom of a deep well,
dark waters at midnight.
Stars reflected perfectly.

Sky Jewelry

Flying in formation—
Obsidian bird-beads,
threaded on invisible strands,

Wild freedom, winged grace;
a one-of-a-kind necklace.

Cloud-sailing, loose ends trailing—
they rise, adorning the neck of the sky.

When It Rains

When it rains,
the world softens
around the edges;
streets and sidewalks
become a liquid mirror
onto which lights
and colors bleed.
When it rains,
everything
becomes beautiful . . .
for a while.

Sacred Hush

There was a special sort of stillness
heavy with hidden meaning.
The trees settled their leaves
and birds silenced their songs,
as if the world had held its breath,
pausing in eager anticipation
of some momentous event.
Alas, I, not being privy to the secret,
could only watch —and wonder.

Fallen Splendor

Rebellious leaves
going out in a blaze of glory,
setting trees aflame
in riotous color.
Reluctant surrender
to rumors of coming winter.
Crisp nights
and insistent winds
pry loose their desperate grip.
One by one,
they learn the art of letting go.
Their final descent
paints the ground lavishly.

The Gray Wolves of Winter

Low clouds lope in silently—
ragged gray wolves of winter.
A snowy devouring,
leaving behind
the gleaming whiteness
of bones licked clean.

What Wild Creatures Know

Unseen in their flight,
wild geese faintly call,
passing high overhead,
in the depths of night.
Instinctive travelers,
on invisible highways.
I envy their lack of lostness.

Dung beetles steer by starlight,
salmon seek spawning rivers by smell,
while birds follow magnetic fields.

Wild creatures somehow know
where they must go, but we—
we humans wander
the paths of confusion.
Trying to be so many things
other than our true selves.
Vagabond hearts,
seeking a place of belonging.
Longing for the home we never knew.

Time Triptych

Time is both
a friend and enemy.
Alpha and omega—
possibility and finality.

Time is the ultimate revealer,
stripping away our lies and illusions,
leaving the bones of truth exposed.

With fraying DNA,
and moth-eaten memories,
we circle in Time's labyrinth,
back to the place of helpless dependence,
finding a kinship of beginnings and endings.

Matches

Our lives
are like matches
in the hand of Time.
Struck at birth,
and held up to light
the darkness.

And when we finally
burn down
to its fingertips,
Time reluctantly
shakes us free,
letting us go.

Time Wounds All Heels

Our journey is a mystery.
Where your road or mine leads,
I cannot say, but this I do know:
Time wounds all heels.
If you don't understand that now,
one day you most certainly will.

In life's dark seasons, we walk sorrow's path.
Reluctantly reaching to pluck
thorn-guarded berries, with trembling hands.
Bright blood droplets appear.
A bouquet of tiny rubies blooming
from the lacerated skin of illusions.
Unwilling though we may be,
bittersweet truths will be tasted,
our lips left stained and bruised.

Life often teaches us more than we care to know.
The well-traveled soul, bearing wisdom's scars
is often reluctant to speak.
For the weighty truth of things is felt marrow-deep.
It does not always fall easily from the tongue.
We shoulder the burden in silence.
Put one foot in front of the other, limping on.

The Love of Fading Things

What is it about me
that loves the minor key
and indigo blue?
Why do I find beautiful,
forgotten weathered barns
that hunch like gaunt old men
bowed by the weight of years?

I like tattered books
with loose bindings,
and sad, bleak stories
tinged with faint hopefulness.

Give me the scattered riches
of discarded autumn leaves
crunching underfoot
like brittle bones of summer.

The lonely whine of the wind
nosing about, seeking cracks in walls,
and the distant laments of a night train
are songs that soothe my soul.

Doesn't it seem that love tastes sweeter,
as we near the bottom of the bottle?

Moon Gold on Dark Waters

The poetry I love best
has words that glimmer
like moon gold
on dark waters,
and a hidden undertow
which pulls me into
its delicate sadness.

The Indefinable Ache

Longing calls out,
like the wild coyote song
which sets stars trembling.

It is the sap of our soul,
rising to meet spring.

The indefinable ache
of a beautiful wound.

Moving moth-winged in darkness,
it brushes against our true face.
By its sacred touch, we are blessed.

What the Night Sees

Night is a shameless voyeur,
peeping through soul windows.
Silent tears and prowling fears.
Lonely hearts howl at the moon
while lovers whisper drunkenly.
Decadent dreamscapes of desire
and bitter truth stripped of illusion;
the human carousel whirls in darkness.
We have an intimacy with Night
that Day knows nothing of.
Masks on the nightstand,
personas hung in the closet,
we are at our most naked
while the sun is sleeping.

Vanishing Footprints

A winter's walk,
late at night.
Dreamlike,
not a soul in sight.
As quiet as death,
the pale ghost
of breath hovers near.
A spirit seeking escape,
yet tethered to my body.

Each streetlight glow,
an oasis in the vast dark.
Every snowflake,
a tiny masterpiece,
pale as angel bones.

This intimate silence
is a holy hush,
holding me like a lover.

The way ahead,
unmarred white.
Fast-falling flakes
will soon erase
all signs of my passing.
I must keep moving,
a few paces ahead of oblivion.

Beneath the Starry Ocean

A pale cheddar moon sails
high above the lonely pines.
Campfire sparks ascend,
rejoining the ocean of stars.
You and I, tiny in the night,
neither of us saying anything.
Hushed by feelings too vast
for the smallness of words.

Sinking into Sweet Darkness

And will the universe
one day collapse,
like a lover spent
after reaching
the pinnacle of passion?

Will it gather
into itself,
the way the sea
calls back a wave?

Will star-sparks subside,
sinking into sweet darkness,
beauty sleeping,
only to reawaken
in some new guise?

Dream Within a Dream

We surrender each night,
slowly sinking down
into a deep sea of sleep,
trusting that we will surface
with the new day's dawning.

We dream within a dream.
One the universe had long, long ago—
a dream which has not yet ended.

A Way of Being in the World

"But what is the meaning," you ask,
arms thrown wide for emphasis,
"of life, the universe . . . everything?"
And I think, what a singular question.
Why just one meaning?
Why not *meanings*?
That "s" changes everything.

What meaning does a blank canvas have?
Ask a painter and she will show you.
Ask another—see what he will paint.
Ask a hundred painters.
Ask thousands upon thousands.
Billions.
We are The Many.
Humanity—a gallery of meanings.

Meaning is something to be
uncovered and discovered.
A way of being in the world.
We are both artist,
and work in progress.
We are the meaning-makers;
bringers-forth-from-within.

The blank canvas of days stretches before us.
What meaning will we fill them with?
Will the final unveiling reveal a masterpiece?

The Long Journey Home

The years since your first cries greeted this world have been filled with false guides and spurious maps. They have led you on a wild goose chase of a journey, far from your true self. But now, after long eating the bread of lies, hunger has sent you circling back in search of what you have left behind. Looking in the mirrored eyes of the stranger you've become, you see the glimmer of something hidden deep within. The familiar child which had been pushed aside, stepping hesitantly from the shadowy depths. Now ready to be embraced in the arms of your older world-weary self. And from this whole-making reunion, will emerge a new self. An amalgam of childlike wonder and hard-fought wisdom. Fresh vision, and a passion for a boldly authentic life.

Between Breaths

This life that we lead
is enclosed between breaths;
from a newborn's first cry
to the last sigh of death.
Since none of us know
just how long that will be,
in this *now* where you are,
live fully and free.

Rare Honey

Refusing to be a beggar
outside Fate's door,
I've stolen rare honey
from the hive of Time.
In the falling drift of days
between cradle and grave,
I've claimed what's mine.
Making peace with myself,
defending happiness
amidst Sorrow's unending war.

Defiance

We ascend the night,
like Chinese lanterns.
Our fragile hearts
carrying Love's flame.
Bravely glowing
despite our knowing
that the darkness will
reclaim us once again.

Time Has Flown

I blinked my eyes
and in an instant,
decades had passed.
Like a brief sunset moment
when clouds on the horizon
are glorious and electric,
then the sun slips away,
and all colors are swallowed
down the thirsty throat of night.

The Dust of Dreams

There is a fragility
to these beautiful moments.
We are pierced by the knowledge
that one day they will only be memories,
frail as dried butterfly wings,
which Time's rough hands crumble
into pigmented powder.

And what of us,
born of star-hearts
and improbability?
We too shall crumble,
becoming the dust
of dreams the universe once had.

Forgetting our form,
we'll rejoin the endless dance,
only to be revealed
and remembered in new ways
in a future unknown to us.

What the Blind Man Heard

I'm no visionary or virtuoso,
not the keeper of deep secrets.
Just a blind man transcribing music
that drifts softly from another room.
I listen to Life's silent song, and take notes.

Crazy Dreamer

I dream of a place
where every orphaned love
finds a welcoming home.

A land where old regrets
are granted second chances,
and cold rivers of sorrow
eventually find their way
to a vast, warm sea of joy.

A country where bruised
and battered hopes
are kissed to life again.

A universe where
entangled hearts
never have to part,
and light swallows up
every last bit of darkness
in the end.

The shadows deepen,
as do these lines on my face.
I'm just a fool with a pen,
and dreams of better things.
Trying to unbreak
the weary heart of the world.

A Noble Intention

Let each dawn be sacred,
every awakening from sleep miraculous.
Let each heartbeat be a holy thing,
each breath a whisper of gratitude.
Let each step be an adventure,
the faces we see, a beautiful mosaic of humanity.
Let our hearts be chalices of love,
may our hands be helpful and empty of hate.
Let deep joy sustain us, and sorrows instruct.
May our eyes find the hidden beauty in all things.

Rusty Eyes

Scrape away the rust
from these jaded eyes
and let me see again
the wild wonder of life;
to know in joy and pain
what a miracle it is
to feel anything at all.
Let me not forget this
before the curtain falls—
to be furiously passionate,
compassionate and curious.
A human, who is truly alive.

Open your heart
and taste
the wild wonder
of life.

Now is the beginning
of everything else.

About the Author

John Mark Green is an IT geek by profession and a writer by passion. His articles and poems have appeared in publications such as the Wittenburg Door, River Poets Journal, Tuck Magazine, Full Moon Rising, The Urban Howl, Thought Catalog, Psychology Today, and more. His poem Burn Our Masks at Midnight appears in the international bestselling book Leadership from the Inside Out by Kevin Cashman. While initially writing poetry as a form of self-reflection, he soon found a growing audience on social media who could relate to his words. He sees poetry as lens through which he can better understand the joys, sorrows, and mysteries of life. John currently resides in Arizona and is in a long-distance relationship with the love of his life, Canadian poet Christy Ann Martine. His next book will be a collection of stories and poems called Tales of an Inconvenient Heart.

Facebook.com/johnmarkgreenpoetry
Instagram.com/johnmarkgreenpoetry
Twitter: @JohnGreenpoetry
www.etsy.com/shop/JohnMarkGreen

About the Artist

Beth Little has been an artist all her life, and she works primarily in watercolor, ink, oils, pencil, and charcoal. She has always been drawn to contemporary artwork that employs elements of subtle humor and whimsy. She tries to apply these characteristics in her own work, which runs a wide and oftentimes provocative spectrum, ranging from childish to realistic and everything in between. Her most common themes are space, love, daydreams, birds, and other wildlife. Under her former last name of Jorgensen, she exhibited two major series of oil paintings: Take the Stairs and "buzz and hum." She also published a children's book called "Total Animals." She is currently working on several upcoming watercolor-based projects, and is available to take commissions as well. Beth resides in Roanoke, Virginia, and is always interested in more opportunities to showcase her work. Visit her on the web at daydreamdaredevil.com. She can also be found on Society 6, Etsy, Instagram, and Tumblr under the same handle (daydreamdaredevil).

Coming Next:

Tales of an Inconvenient Heart

A collection of poems and short stories.

Made in United States
Orlando, FL
31 March 2023